CHAIN OF COLONIAL HOUSES

CHAIN OF COLONIAL HOUSES

ANONYMOUS

ISBN: 978-93-5614-680-8

Published: -

LECTOR HOUSE LLP
E-MAIL: info@lectorhouse.com

CHAIN OF COLONIAL HOUSES

BY

ANONYMOUS

CONTENTS

THE ASSOCIATE COMMITTEE OF WOMEN OF THE PENNSYLVANIA MUSEUM OF ART

HONORARY PRESIDENT
Mrs. Rudolph Blankenburg

PRESIDENT
Mrs. Frank Thorne Patterson

VICE-PRESIDENTS
Mrs. H. S. Prentiss Nichols
Mrs. Henry Brinton Coxe
Mrs. Edgar W. Baird
Miss Margaretta S. Hinchman

CORRESPONDING SECRETARY
Mrs. Herbert L. Clark

RECORDING SECRETARY
Mrs. H. Norris Harrison

TREASURER
Mrs. Edward Browning

MEMBERS
Mrs. Lewis Audenried
Mrs. Rudolph Blankenburg
Mrs. William T. Carter
Mrs. E. Bissell Clay
Mrs. S. Grey Dayton
Mrs. William A. Dick
Mrs. Fitz-Eugene Dixon
Mrs. Russell Duane
Miss Louisa Eyre
Mrs. Stanley G. Flagg, Jr.
Mrs. George H. Frazier
Mrs. Henry C. Gibson
Mrs. F. Woodson Hancock
Mrs. Charles Wolcott Henry
Mrs. John S. Jenks
Mrs. Charles F. Judson
Mrs. Robert R. Logan
Mrs. W. Logan MacCoy

Mrs. John C. Martin
Mrs. Sydney E. Martin
Mrs. John D. McIlhenny
Mrs. Richard Waln Meirs
Mrs. Thornton Oakley
Mrs. Henry Norris Platt
Mrs. Eli Kirk Price
Mrs. Logan Rhoads
Mrs. C. Shillard-Smith
Miss Jessie Willcox Smith
Mrs. John B. Stetson
Mrs. W. Standley Stokes
Mrs. William H. Walbaum
Mrs. P. A. B. Widener, 2nd
Mrs. C. Stewart Wurts

HONORARY MEMBERS
Mrs. Hampton L. Carson
Miss Margaret Clyde
Mrs. Henry S. Grove
Mrs. Arthur V. Meigs
Mrs. Edward T. Stotesbury
Mrs. M. Hampton Todd
Mrs. Percival Roberts, Jr.

PHILADELPHIA HOUSES
IN COLONIAL TIMES

Philadelphia was the most important city in the colonies and the home of many leaders of thought and action in the days which saw the birth of the American nation. We are fortunate in having preserved for us the few historic landmarks in Fairmount Park, which have been restored through the leadership of the Pennsylvania Museum of Art and cooperative institutions and by the generosity of Philadelphians. This book contains pictures and sketches of eight old colonial houses, several of which date back to the middle of the eighteenth century.

Of the houses described, Cedar Grove, Belmont, The Cliffs, Woodford and Mount Pleasant antedate the Revolution, and are examples of early Georgian and mid-Georgian styles. The simple stone cottages which stand on the grounds at Belmont, Woodford and Strawberry antedate in style the mansion-houses there. Even the oldest portion of Cedar Grove, 1721, already shows a front of squared masonry, while the oldest part of Woodford has on the end the glazed headers which characterize the earliest brick buildings of the colony. The later houses are generally covered with stucco.

By the middle of the century there were bold classic doorways, as at Belmont, Woodford (then enlarged) and Mount Pleasant. Rich ornamented ceilings from about 1760 are found at Belmont; the principal rooms at Woodford and Mount Pleasant are adorned with elaborate carving in the Chippendale style. After the Revolution the more slender proportions of the Adam style were adopted, in the later part of Cedar Grove and at Lemon Hill, Sweetbrier and Strawberry. The wings at Strawberry show the severe classic detail of the Greek Revival.

SWEETBRIER, 1797

Shown on map as No. 1

SWEETBRIER

The first owner of Sweetbrier was Samuel Breck, who records in his notes that he built his mansion in 1797, having "out-buildings of every kind suitable for elegance and comfort. The prospect consists of the river, animated by its great trade carried on in boats of about thirty tons, drawn by horses; of a beautiful sloping lawn, terminating at that river, now nearly four hundred yards wide opposite the portico; of side-screen woods; of gardens, green-house, etc.—Sweetbrier is the name of my villa."

The restoration was undertaken in 1918 by the Junior League of Philadelphia, with the advice of the Museum, and the house now serves as the headquarters for the Junior League.

On entering, the visitor will be impressed with the simplicity of the architecture and the delicacy of the ornament. Of a later date than that of Mount Pleasant, the style is more classic, varied by the relief ornament of the mantels and the number of large graceful windows. The large reception room contains four beautifully carved Heppelwhite side chairs, a pair of mahogany card tables and a sofa of the same style. Wedgwood vases, gilt torchères and a large Oriental rug represent imported objects which the room might have exhibited in its original state. A rare acquisition, a complete set of William Birch's views of Philadelphia, hang upon these walls and on the stair landing. At the right of the fireplace stands a painted armchair with needlepoint back and seat, and nearby is a tripod candlestand. These pieces formed a part of the original furnishings of Sweetbrier, and have been lent by the descendants of Samuel Breck. In a vitrine near the west door, a miniature on ivory shows the youthful Samuel Breck.

CEDAR GROVE, 1721-1795

Shown on map as No. 2

CEDAR GROVE

Cedar Grove is an ancestral home of the Morris family. The house, which stood for over two hundred years near Harrowgate station in Frankford, in 1927 was removed stone by stone. It has been re-erected on Lansdowne Drive near Memorial Hall, with its original contents, through the generosity of Miss Lydia Thompson Morris. The land at Frankford was bought in 1714 by Thomas Coates of High Street, the father of Elizabeth Coates. In 1721 Elizabeth married Isaac Paschall, and it is from this time that dates the oldest portion of the house. Isaac Paschall, a son of Elizabeth, married Patience Mifflin in 1767. The house came to his daughter Sarah, who married Isaac W. Morris in 1795.

Through the munificent gift of Miss Morris, Cedar Grove has retained its heirlooms dating from 1720 to 1800. Within its walls may be seen furniture from the simple William and Mary type to the elegant examples of Heppelwhite and Sheraton.

One enters directly into the living room with the informality of pre-Revolutionary times. The Chippendale sofa, upholstered in yellow brocade, the pie-crust table and the six ball-and-claw foot chairs combine easily with the earlier William and Mary highboy and lowboy.

In the dining room, the majority of pieces illustrate the formal Heppelwhite style. The kitchen remains in a simple state, its large fireplace adequately supplied with cranes and pots.

Passing upstairs one visits the several bedrooms, furnished mainly in Heppelwhite style. The beds with their fluted posts and straight chintz hangings illustrate the simplicity which followed Chippendale's exuberant curves. In the same style are mahogany chests of drawers with bracket feet.

BELMONT, 1755

Shown on map as No. 3

BELMONT

Belmont was the product of gradual growth. In the stone cottage Judge Richard Peters, the most famous owner of the estate, was born on June 22, 1744. The adjoining brick structure, ultimately forming a south wing of the mansion house, comes next in order of time, 1745. The present main house, of brick and rubble, followed, probably about 1755, and, somewhat later, the great stair tower. The style of their ornaments indicates these were finished about 1760, and we know that by 1762 they stood essentially complete, surrounded by well-developed gardens and plantations.

William Peters, the father of Richard, had come to America in 1739, married Mary Breitnall, and acquired the property by deed of July 21, 1742. It had been from the beginning of the war in the tenancy of Richard Peters, to whom it was finally conveyed in 1786, and was occupied by him until his death in 1828. In 1927 it was restored by Fritz Pflug, restaurateur, with the advice of the Museum.

It represents the early Georgian style of the middle of the eighteenth century, a precursor of the rocaille ornament of the Chippendale period. The massiveness of the carving and plaster ceiling ornaments harks back to motifs common to the late seventeenth century of the Louis XIV style.

The contents of the older part of the house are copies of mid-eighteenth century Philadelphia furniture. In the parlour opposite the fireplace stands a replica of the sofa owned by Washington during his residence in Philadelphia. Above it is to be seen a portrait of William Peters, the builder of Belmont. The ceiling is considered the earliest ornamental plaster work in an American house.

STRAWBERRY, 1798

Shown on map as No. 4

STRAWBERRY

Strawberry's first owner, in 1798, was Judge Lewis, a notable lawyer and a member of the Pennsylvania Assembly.

The original house was of the then new American style with certain light touches reminiscent of the Adam period, the entrance hall having four niches and gouged mouldings. The wings in the taste of the Greek Revival were added about 1825 by the second owner Judge Joseph Hemphill, a close friend of Jefferson and an ardent democrat. Lafayette was among the many distinguished guests entertained at Strawberry during the second period of the house.

Strawberry has been restored by the Committee of 1926, a group of women who were instrumental in building High Street at the Sesquicentennial Celebration.

The furniture at Strawberry is of the late eighteenth and first quarter of the nineteenth centuries. In the parlour a fine Sheraton sofa and four chairs are noteworthy, as is the piano made in Philadelphia by Charles Albrecht in 1785. Across the hall, the library is consistently furnished in the Empire style. A fine writing desk with rounded ends, a Regency suite of black settee and armchairs with X-shaped supports and four gilt chairs are noteworthy pieces.

Beyond is the Music Room, its windows and mantel forming the decorative features of the room. Upstairs are two late eighteenth century rooms. One shows a fine Heppelwhite sideboard and a set of Sheraton chairs, the other a carved four-post bed, "Beau-Brummel" toilet chest and Sheraton chairs. Beyond is a small Empire bedroom.

In the opposite wing the Banquet Room is carried out in the same manner, the star-sprinkled walls, crystal and bronze chandelier and imperial yellow silk draperies having the formality of the First Empire.

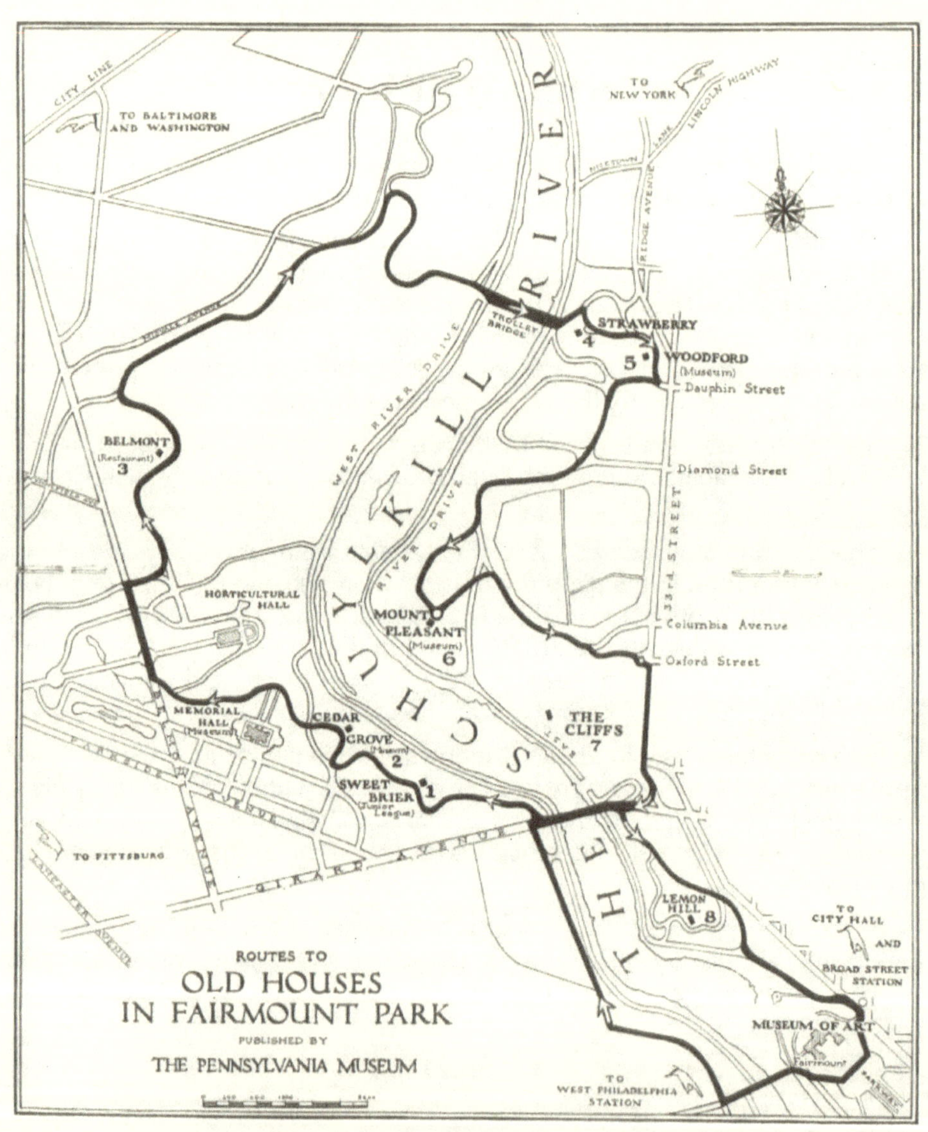

ROUTES TO OLD HOUSES IN FAIRMOUNT PARK

PUBLISHED BY *The Pennsylvania Museum*

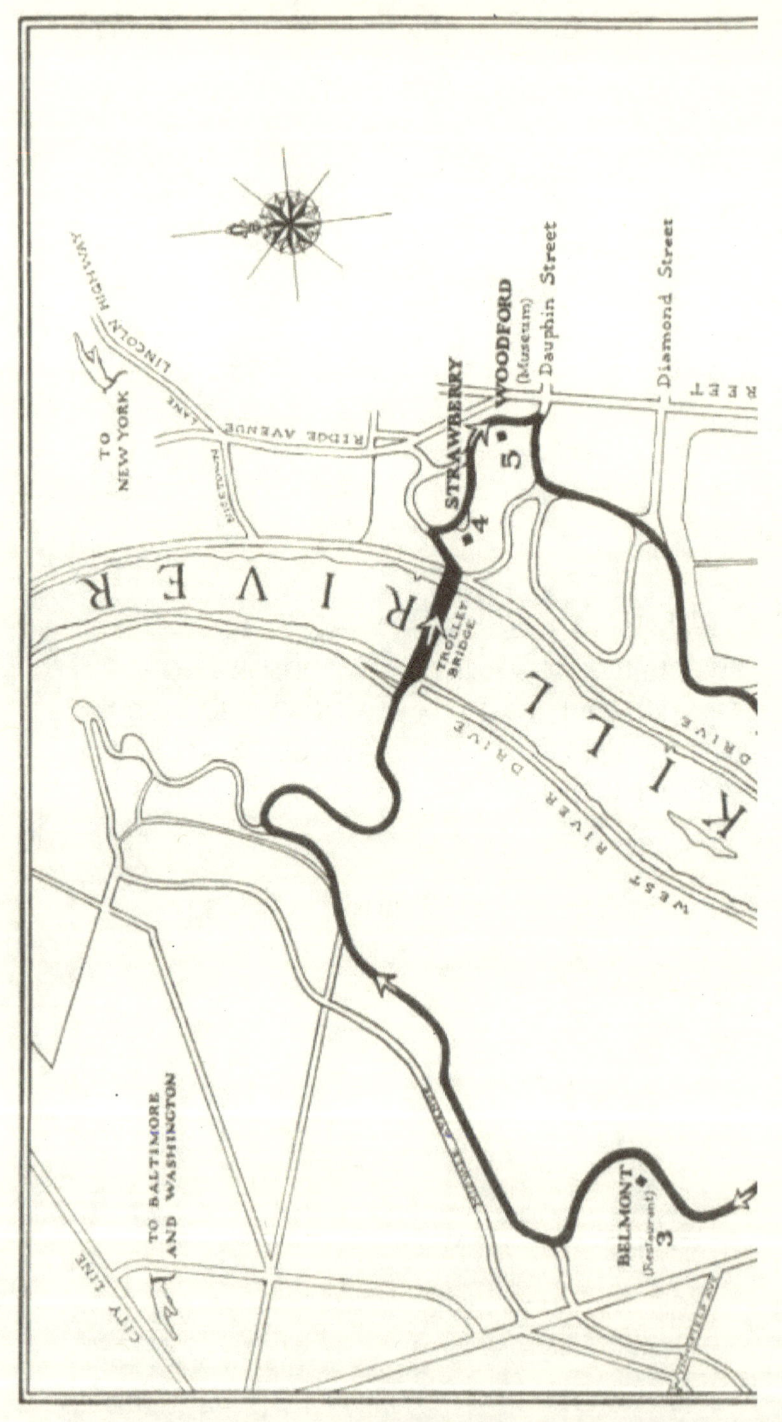

ROUTES TO OLD HOUSES IN FAIRMOUNT PARK (*Enlarged - Top*)

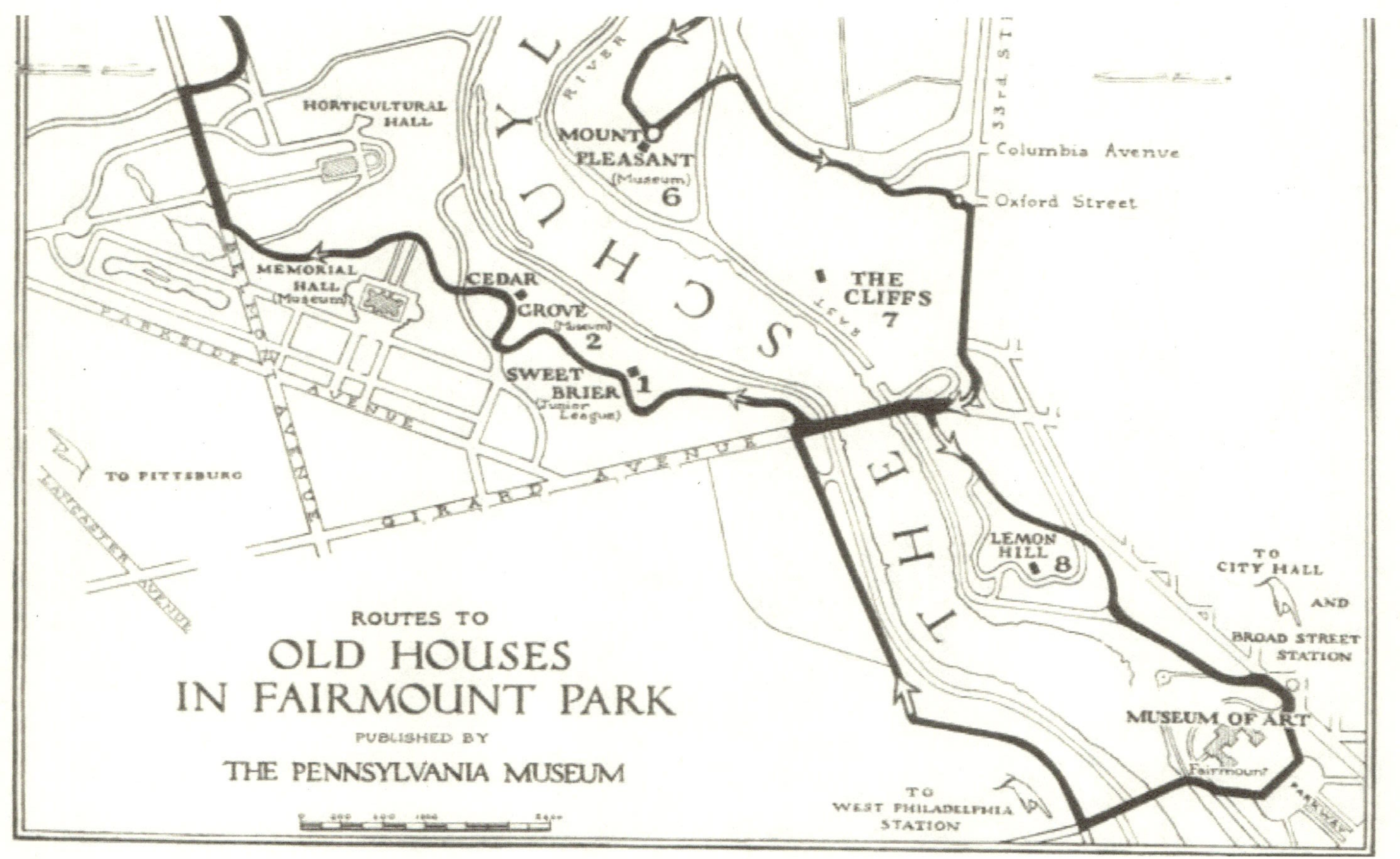

ROUTES TO OLD HOUSES IN FAIRMOUNT PARK (*Enlarged - Bottom*)

WOODFORD, 1756

Shown on map as No. 5

WOODFORD

Woodford has long been distinguished for its stately proportions, tawny yellow brickwork and many-paned windows, behind a screen of beautiful walnut trees. It has lately been opened to the public by Daniel T. V. Huntoon, Trustee of the estate of the late Naomi Wood. Her bequest of her collection together with an endowment fund, has been the means of accomplishing this restoration.

The early history of Woodford is not definitely known, as there were nine changes of ownership from 1693, when the original grant of land was made by William Penn, to 1800.

On entering the house the visitor finds the hall distinguished by a panelled wainscot, fluted pilasters and six doors. To the left is the parlour, one of the handsomest rooms of the period in America.

Amongst the furniture, which is American throughout, are a rare Chippendale sofa and wing chair, a fine example of the transitional style of armchair, a small writing desk of about 1690, and a Philadelphia tripod tea-table.

The lighting fixtures are rare examples of authentic metalwork, the brass chandelier having come from England about 1725. A pair of George II gilt bronze wall sconces between the windows came from Hornby Castle in Yorkshire.

Across the hall, the dining room is a counterpart of the parlour save for the chimneypiece and furniture. On leaving the dining room, the staircase is evident for the first time, as it occupies the wing added upon the completion of the house in 1756. Above the stairs are two large rooms and a smaller room. Over the parlour is the master's bedroom, now restored as a sitting room. Some pieces of furniture in this room go back to 1700. In the bedroom upon the walnut highboy are old bandboxes covered with stencilled papers.

MOUNT PLEASANT, 1761

Shown on map as No. 6

MOUNT PLEASANT

The mansion built in 1761 by John Macpherson was sold on March 27, 1779, to Benedict Arnold. Keeping a life interest himself, he settled it, as his marriage gift, on his beautiful bride, the heiress Peggy Shippen, daughter of Edward Shippen. Benedict Arnold never occupied it. Later his life interest was confiscated and the mansion was sold in 1781. Edward Shippen ultimately consolidated the entire ownership in his family by purchase in 1784. Meanwhile the house had had another distinguished tenant, if not occupant, in Major General Baron von Steuben. Later it was sold to General Jonathan Williams, in whose family it remained until 1853. In 1926 it was restored through the generosity of the late Charles H. Ludington.

The atmosphere of a Revolutionary house has been created by finishing the rooms with Chippendale furniture, contemporary portraits, and small objects of foreign importation.

The entrance is simply furnished with a Georgian mirror and table. In the large and formal parlour at the right stands a very handsome secretary bookcase originally made in the City. Fitting companions to this piece, a beautifully carved highboy, tripod table and chairs in the Philadelphia Chippendale style, give the room an air of elegance. On the stair landing stands a tall clock bearing the name of "David Rittenhouse," the most famous clockmaker in America.

On the second floor, two bedrooms are attractively furnished with four-post beds and hung, to match the windows, with appropriate India prints and eighteenth century Chintz. Pieces by Philadelphia cabinetmakers bear evidence to the excellent qualities of their workmanship. Other noteworthy pieces are two fine wing chairs, a block-front desk and a pair of ladder-back chairs.

THE CLIFFS, 1741

Shown on map as No. 7

THE CLIFFS

The Cliffs stands above the East River Drive, commanding a splendid view down the Schuylkill to the south toward Lemon Hill, and to the north past Mount Pleasant. The house, a compact structure of stuccoed rubble, was built by Samuel Rowland Fisher in 1741 and, unlike several other of the park houses in the Museum group, remained in the ownership of one family until taken over by the Park Commission in 1868. It had, however, been leased from time to time, as a letter dated 1789 bears witness, written by Sarah Bache to Benjamin Franklin, her father, who was then in France. It relates that she had just moved to "this small, charming house which the French minister (who is delivering letter) will describe in detail."

There is considerable panelling of a simple kind throughout the house, chiefly occurring on the chimney wall of the rooms, the remaining walls being plastered and wainscoted. The parlour, opening directly from the outside, is a dignified room having exposures on two sides and a panelled chimney wall on the third.

The Cliffs is not usually open to the public. Mr. and Mrs. Erling H. Pedersen, the occupants, have gathered many old pieces of American furniture suitable to the house. Particularly notable is a slant-top walnut desk, a small Chippendale sofa and a pair of ladder-back side chairs. Beyond is the dining room, one stair leading down into the old kitchen with its great fireplace and beamed ceiling, the other leading up to two pleasant chambers, furnished with four-post beds and early walnut chests of drawers.

LEMON HILL, 1798

Shown on map as No. 8

LEMON HILL

Lemon Hill was built in 1798 on the site of the Robert Morris country house called "The Hills." Here he had his famous green houses with the first lemon trees in Philadelphia, which ultimately gave their name to the estate.

On Morris' insolvency it was purchased by Henry Pratt, an opulent merchant, who built the present house. The oval drawing room was of the type then popular among the leaders of the government and society, found also in the White House in Washington and in the homes of Alexander Hamilton and General Henry Knox. The drawing room on the first floor and dining room on the floor below are the principal rooms of the house, the long windows on the south side giving a prospect of the river and being balanced on the opposite wall by a pair of fireplaces. The curved mahogany doors in these rooms are rich accents of colour against the blue woodwork and buff walls. In the library is one of the most delicate and beautiful of the early marble mantelpieces, with the legend of Leda.

Mr. and Mrs. Fiske Kimball, who occupy the house, have furnished it with appropriate pieces of the late eighteenth century in the Heppelwhite and Sheraton style. In the drawing room is a handsome suite of white and gold furniture in the Louis XVI style, including a settee and twelve armchairs. They were made in Philadelphia about 1800 for Edward Burd. The hangings are of a classic pattern in blue and silver, and over the mantels are a pair of colourful landscapes in the manner of Hubert Robert.

BUS AND TROLLEY ROUTES

ROUTE A — ROOSEVELT BOULEVARD

Southbound: From Frankford ave. and Pratt st., on Pratt st., Roosevelt blvd., Hunting Park ave., 29th st., Chalmers ave., Lehigh ave., 33rd st., Sedgeley Drive, Lemon Hill Drive, Fairmount ave., Pennsylvania ave., 23rd st., Parkway, Race st., Broad st., to Broad and Filbert sts.

Northbound: From Broad and Filbert sts., on Filbert st., Parkway, 23rd st., Pennsylvania ave., Fairmount ave., Lemon Hill Drive, Sedgeley Drive, 33rd st., Lehigh ave., Chalmers ave., 29th st., Hunting Park ave., Roosevelt blvd., Pratt st., to Frankford ave. and Pratt st.

ROUTE 9 — STRAWBERRY — FOURTH AND FIFTH

Southbound: From 32nd st. and Ridge ave., on 32nd st., Columbia ave., 19th st., Poplar st., 18th st., Brown st., 22nd st., Arch st., 4th st., Ritner st., to 5th and Ritner sts.

Northbound: From 5th and Ritner sts., on 5th st., Arch st., 23rd st., Aspen st., 27th st., Poplar st., 29th st., Columbia ave., 31st st., York st., 32nd st., to 32nd st. and Ridge ave.

ROUTE 61 — MANAYUNK

Southbound: From Main st. and Leverington ave. (Manayunk), on Main st., Ridge ave., 15th st., Wallace st., 10th st., to 9th and Spruce sts.

Northbound: From 9th and Spruce sts., on 9th st., Spring Garden st., 8th st., Fairmount ave., Ridge ave., Main st., to Main st. and Leverington ave.

ROUTE 54 — LEHIGH AVE.

Eastbound: From 34th and Huntingdon sts., on Huntingdon st., Ridge ave., Lehigh ave., Kensington ave., Somerset st., Edgemont st., Cambria st., to Richmond and Cambria sts.

Westbound: From Richmond and Cambria sts., on Richmond st., Somerset st., Kensington ave., Lehigh ave, 34th st., to 34th and Huntingdon sts.

ROUTE 39 — DAUPHIN AND SUSQUEHANNA

Eastbound: From 33rd and Dauphin sts., on Dauphin st., Front st., Kensington ave., Cumberland st., to Richmond and Cumberland sts.

Westbound: From Richmond and Cumberland sts., on Richmond st., Huntingdon st., Kensington ave., Front st., Susquehanna ave., 21st st., York st., 33rd st., to 33rd and Dauphin sts.

ROUTE 8—DAUPHIN AND SUSQUEHANNA

Eastbound: From 33rd and Dauphin sts., on Dauphin st., Front st., Norris st., Susquehanna ave., Richmond st., to Richmond and Norris sts.

Westbound: From Richmond and Norris sts., on Norris st., Susquehanna ave., 21st st., York st., 33rd st., to 33rd and Dauphin sts.

ROUTE 7—STRAWBERRY—TWENTY-SECOND AND TWENTY-THIRD

Southbound: From 33rd and Dauphin sts., on Dauphin st., 29th st., Poplar st., 28th st., Brown st., 22nd st., Snyder ave., to 23rd st. and Snyder ave.

Northbound: From 23rd st. and Snyder ave., on 23rd st., Aspen st., 27th st., Poplar st., 29th st., York st., 33rd st., to 33rd and Dauphin sts.

ROUTE 70—FIFTY-SECOND ST.—BALA

Southbound: From City Line (Bala), on 54th st., Jefferson st., 52nd st., Baltimore ave., 49th st., Saybrook ave., Hanson st., Paschall ave., to 49th st. and Paschall ave.

Northbound: From 49th st. and Paschall ave., on 49th st., Baltimore ave., 52nd st., Jefferson st., 54th st., to City Line.

ROUTE 38A—52ND ST. EXTENSION

Eastbound: From 52nd and Jefferson sts., on 52nd st., Parkside ave., to 40th st. and Parkside ave.

Westbound: From 40th st. and Parkside ave., on Parkside ave., 52nd st., to 52nd and Jefferson sts.

ROUTE 38—BARING—SUBWAY-SURFACE

Eastbound: From 44th st. and Parkside ave. Loop, on Parkside ave., 40th st., Fairmount ave., 37th st., Baring st., 33rd st., Lancaster ave., Market st., in Subway to City Hall.

Westbound: From City Hall in Subway to Market st. (surface), on Market st., Lancaster ave., 33rd st., Baring st., 36th st., Fairmount ave., 40th st., Parkside ave., to 44th st. and Parkside ave. Loop.

ROUTE 40—LOMBARD AND SOUTH

Eastbound: From 41st and Parkside ave., on Parkside ave., 40th st., Spruce st., South st., 17th st., Lombard st., to Front and Lombard sts.

Westbound: From Front and Lombard sts., on Front st., South st., Spruce st., 38th st., Market st., 41st st., Ogden st., 40th st., Girard ave., 41st st., to 41st st. and Parkside ave.

Lector House believes that a society develops through a two-fold approach of continuous learning and adaptation, which is derived from the study of classic literary works spread across the historic timeline of literature records. Therefore, we aim at reviving, repairing and redeveloping all those inaccessible or damaged but historically as well as culturally important literature across subjects so that the future generations may have an opportunity to study and learn from past works to embark upon a journey of creating a better future.

This book is a result of an effort made by Lector House towards making a contribution to the preservation and repair of original ancient works which might hold historical significance to the approach of continuous learning across subjects.

HAPPY READING & LEARNING!

LECTOR HOUSE LLP
E-MAIL: info@lectorhouse.com